From Broke to

Boss: The Complete Manual

for Achieving Financial Independence Through Internet Revenue

By:

LUMAH H.

Introduction

Are you tired of living paycheck to paycheck? Are you bored of the monotony of a 9-to-5 job and the limitations it imposes on your financial freedom? Do you envision waking up every morning excited because you know you have control over your financial situation?

If so, you're not alone. Millions of individuals worldwide are locked in a vicious cycle of debt, bills, and financial stress. What if I told you there was a way to break the pattern and attain financial independence?

Thank you for downloading "From Broke to Boss: The Complete Manual for Achieving Financial Independence Through Internet Revenue". This book will help you alter your financial life and establish a future filled with success, independence, and peace of mind.

In the following pages, we will delve into the realm of online income and show you how to earn various streams of cash, putting you on the path to financial freedom. We'll go over everything from affiliate marketing to online sales of items and services.

However, this book is more than just a guide to making money online. It's a complete book that will show you how to launch a successful internet business, grow a dedicated following, and greatly raise your revenue.

So, if you're ready to take control of your finances and begin enjoying the life you've always desired, this book is for you. Let us go on this journey to financial independence together!

This book will teach you the following:

How to create several streams of internet income.

How to Build a Successful Online Business.

How to establish a loyal following while increasing your revenue.

How to overcome normal challenges while remaining motivated.

And much more!

Prepare to alter your financial situation!

Turn the page, and let's get started on your path to financial freedom now!

Chapter 1: Breaking Free from Financial Struggles

Welcome to the first chapter of "From Broke to Boss: The Complete Manual for Achieving Financial Independence Through Internet Revenue". In this chapter, we will look at the existing financial position, identify the causes of financial difficulties, define financial goals, and construct a vision for financial freedom.

Understanding the current financial situation.

Before we can begin to plan for financial freedom, we must first comprehend our current financial status. This includes:

Income: How much do you make per month?

Expenses: How much do you spend each month on bills, rent, and other necessities?

Debt: Do you have any debt, such as credit cards, student loans, or other sorts of debt?

Do you have any savings or emergency funds?

Understanding your present financial condition will help you find areas where you may make improvements to enhance your financial health.

Identifying Reasons for Financial Struggles

Once you've determined your current financial status, it's time to figure out why you're struggling. Some common reasons for financial troubles are:

Lack of financial education: Many people struggle financially because they do not understand personal finance or money management.

Overspending: Spending too much money on non-essential products can soon cause financial problems.

Debt: High amounts of debt, such as credit card debt and student loans, can be a significant impediment to financial independence.

Lack of income: Not having a consistent income or generating enough money can make it harder to obtain financial independence.

By recognizing the causes of your financial difficulties, you may begin to devise solutions for overcoming these obstacles and obtaining financial freedom.

Setting Financial Goals and Developing a Vision for Financial Freedom

Now that you understand your current financial condition and have recognized the causes of your financial difficulties, it's time to set financial goals and create a vision for financial independence. This includes:

Short-term goals: What do you hope to accomplish in the next 6-12 months? This could include paying off debt, setting up an emergency fund, or increasing your income.

Long-term goals: What do you hope to accomplish over the next 1-5 years? This could entail purchasing a home, launching a business, or reaching financial freedom.

Vision of financial freedom: What exactly does financial freedom mean to you? What kind of lifestyle do you hope to have? What kind of financial security do you hope to achieve?

Setting financial goals and building a vision for financial freedom can help you develop a plan for attaining your financial goals and creating a more secure and prosperous future.

In this chapter, we examined the existing financial condition, identified the causes of financial difficulties, established financial goals, and developed a vision for financial freedom. Understanding your current financial state, identifying the causes of your financial difficulties, and setting financial goals can help you develop a strategy for reaching financial independence and creating a more secure and prosperous financial future.

Key Takeaways

Understanding your existing financial condition is essential for gaining financial freedom.

Identifying the causes of your financial difficulties will help you build methods for overcoming them.

Setting financial goals and seeing financial independence might help you create a strategy for reaching your financial goals.

Action Items

Examine your present financial condition, including income, expenses, debt, and savings.

Determine the root causes of your financial problems and devise solutions to overcome them.

Set financial goals and develop a vision for financial freedom, encompassing short-term and long-term objectives, as well as a vision for your perfect financial future.

Chapter 2: The Power of Online Income

Welcome to the second part of "From Broke to Boss: The Complete Manual for Achieving Financial Independence Through Internet Revenue". In this chapter, we'll look at the power of online revenue, including the benefits, success stories of people who have achieved financial independence through online income, and an overview of online income streams.

Introduction to Online Income Streams

Online revenue streams relate to the different methods by which people can make money via the internet. This may include:

Freelancing entails providing services such as writing, design, and programming through freelance platforms such as Upwork or Fiverr.

Affiliate marketing is the practice of promoting other companies' products or services in exchange for a commission on purchases.

Selling products online entails selling physical or digital things using online marketplaces such as Amazon or Etsy.

Creating and marketing online classes in areas including cooking, photography, and coding.

Blogging is the practice of creating a blog and monetizing it through advertising, affiliate marketing, or sponsored content.

These are just a few examples of internet revenue streams; there are plenty of other options accessible.

Benefits of Online Income

There are several benefits to making money online, including:

Flexibility: Online income can be produced from any place with an internet connection, providing for a more flexible work schedule and location.

Scalability: Online income can be increased or decreased according to an individual's requirements and ambitions.

Autonomy: Online income can give people the opportunity to work independently and make their own choices.

Potential for passive income: Some online income streams, such as affiliate marketing or digital product sales, can generate passive income.

These characteristics make Internet income an appealing choice for people trying to achieve financial independence.

Success Stories of People Who Have Achieved Financial Independence via Online Income

There are numerous success stories about people who have attained financial independence through online revenue. Here are some instances.

Michelle Schroeder-Gardner: Michelle is a blogger who earns more than $100,000 per month via affiliate marketing and sponsored posts.

Pat Flynn is a writer and podcaster who makes more than \$100,000 per month from affiliate marketing, sponsored content, and online courses.

Sarah Jones: Sarah is a freelance writer who makes more than \$50,000 per month from freelance writing and affiliate marketing.

These success stories demonstrate how internet income can give financial freedom and a higher quality of life.

In this chapter, we've looked at the power of online revenue, including the benefits, success stories of people who have achieved financial independence through online income, and an overview of online income streams. Individuals who grasp the benefits and potential of online income can begin to construct a plan for obtaining financial independence through it.

Key Takeaways

Online revenue sources offer flexibility, scalability, and autonomy.

There are numerous success stories about people who have attained financial independence through online revenue.

Online revenue can lead to passive income opportunities.

Action Items

Examine various internet revenue streams to uncover prospective prospects.

Create a plan to achieve financial independence through online revenue.

Take action and start creating online revenue sources.

Chapter 3: Creating a Foundation for Online Success

Welcome to the third chapter of "From Broke to Boss: The Complete Manual for Achieving Financial Independence Through Internet Revenue". In this chapter, we'll look at the key elements to laying the groundwork for online success, such as creating a professional online presence, understanding online marketing and sales, cultivating a growth mindset, and overcoming barriers.

Establishing a Professional Online Presence

A professional internet presence is essential for running a successful online business. This includes:

Website development is creating a website that promotes your products or services, provides useful content, and establishes your brand.

Social media: Creating social media profiles that reflect your business and allow you to engage with your target audience.

Email marketing entails establishing an email list and developing email marketing campaigns to nurture your audience and promote your products or services.

Setting up a professional online presence allows you to develop your brand, get trust from your audience, and boost your online visibility.

Understanding Online Marketing and Sales

Understanding internet marketing and sales is critical for establishing a profitable online business. This includes optimizing your website and content for higher search engine rankings (SERPs).

Pay-per-click (PPC) advertising entails creating and managing paid advertising campaigns on platforms such as Google AdWords and Facebook Ads.

Information marketing is the process of creating and distributing valuable information to attract and engage your target audience.

Conversion rate optimization (CRO) entails improving your website and marketing initiatives in order to enhance conversions and sales.

Understanding internet marketing and sales allows you to build successful marketing programs that drive traffic, generate leads, and improve revenue.

Developing a growth mindset and overcoming obstacles

Building a successful Internet business requires a growth attitude and the ability to overcome challenges. This includes:

Embracing failure is viewing it as a chance to learn and improve.

Finding ways to remain motivated and focused on your goals.

Overcoming self-doubt: Developing confidence while overcoming self-doubt

Staying adaptive means being open to new ideas and willing to pivot as required.

Developing a growth mindset and conquering hurdles allows you to remain focused, motivated, and adaptive in the face of challenges and setbacks.

In this chapter, we looked at the key elements to laying the groundwork for online success, such as creating a professional online presence, understanding online marketing and sales, adopting a growth mindset, and overcoming challenges. By taking these steps, you can build a solid foundation for your internet business and position yourself for success.

Key Takeaways

Creating a professional online presence is critical for running a successful online business.

Understanding internet marketing and sales is critical for driving traffic, generating leads, and growing revenue.

Developing a development mentality and conquering hurdles is critical to remaining focused, motivated, and flexible.

Action Items

Create a professional website and social media profiles.

Create a content marketing plan and produce great material.

Begin establishing an email list and launching email marketing campaigns.

Create a growth mentality and discover techniques to stay motivated and focused on your objectives.

Chapter 4: Creating Multiple Income Streams

Welcome to the fourth chapter of "From Broke to Boss: The Complete Manual for Achieving Financial Independence Through Internet Revenue". In this chapter, we'll look at the many internet income streams, tactics for developing numerous income streams, and advice for diversifying income streams and lowering financial risk.

Overview of several online income streams

There are numerous internet income streams that you might pursue, including:

Affiliate marketing is the practice of promoting other companies' products or services in exchange for a commission on purchases.

Selling products: Selling physical or digital goods via online marketplaces such as Amazon or Etsy.

Freelancing entails providing services such as writing, design, and programming through freelance platforms such as Upwork or Fiverr.

Creating and marketing online classes in areas including cooking, photography, and coding.

Blogging is the practice of creating a blog and monetizing it through advertising, affiliate marketing, or sponsored content.

Dividend investing is the practice of investing in stocks that pay dividends to generate a consistent income stream.

Airbnb allows you to rent out a spare room in your house to travelers and tourists.

These are just a few examples of internet revenue streams; there are plenty of other options accessible.

Strategies to Create Multiple Income Streams

Creating various revenue streams allows you to diversify your income and lower your financial risk. Here are some ideas for generating numerous revenue streams:

Begin small: Begin with one or two income streams and gradually increase as you get more comfortable.

Diversify your revenue. Do not put all your eggs in one basket. Diversify your revenue streams to mitigate financial risk.

Concentrate on high-demand areas: Concentrate on regions that are in great demand and have a strong potential for expansion.

Create many income streams simultaneously: Create many income streams simultaneously to boost your chances of success.

Following these tactics can help you generate various income streams and boost your chances of obtaining financial freedom.

Tips to Diversify Income Streams and Reduce Financial Risk

Diversifying your revenue streams and lowering your financial risk can help you reach financial independence. Here are some strategies for diversifying your revenue streams and lowering financial risk:

Don't rely on one revenue source: Do not rely solely on one source of income. Diversify your revenue streams to mitigate financial risk.

To limit your financial risk, diversify your investments into asset classes such as stocks, bonds, and real estate.

Create an emergency fund: Create an emergency fund to cover unexpected expenses and minimize financial risk.

Monitor and manage your income streams. Monitor your revenue sources and alter them as needed to ensure that they remain in line with your financial objectives.

By following these suggestions, you can diversify your income streams and lower your financial risk, boosting your chances of achieving financial independence.

In this chapter, we looked at the various Internet income streams, tactics for developing numerous income streams, and advice for diversifying income streams and lowering financial risk. Follow these ideas and tips to generate various income sources and boost your chances of obtaining financial freedom.

Key Takeaways

You can investigate a variety of online revenue streams.

Creating various revenue streams allows you to diversify your income and lower your financial risk.

Diversifying your revenue streams and lowering your financial risk can help you reach financial independence.

Action Items

Examine various internet revenue streams to uncover prospective prospects.

Make a plan to generate several income streams.

Begin generating various income streams simultaneously.

Monitor and change your income sources as needed to ensure that they remain aligned with your financial objectives.

Chapter 5: Creating A Profitable Online Business

Welcome to the fifth chapter of "From Broke to Boss: The Complete Manual for Achieving Financial Independence Through Internet Revenue". In this chapter, we'll look at the basic elements for starting a profitable online business, such as making a business plan and defining goals, evaluating target markets and customer demands, and developing a sales funnel and marketing strategy.

Developing a Business Plan and Setting Goals

Developing a business strategy and setting goals are critical for establishing a lucrative internet business. This includes:

Define your mission and vision: Define your purpose and vision statements to help guide your business decisions.

Conducting market research is essential for understanding your target market and client needs.

Setting Financial Goals: Establishing financial objectives, such as revenue and profit targets.

Develop a marketing strategy to reach your target market and meet your financial objectives.

By developing a business plan and setting goals, you can set a clear course for your online business and make educated decisions to drive development and profitability.

Understanding Target Markets and Customers' Needs

Understanding your target market and client needs is critical to establishing a lucrative internet business. This includes:

Identifying Your Target Market: Identifying and comprehending your target audience's demographics, needs, and pain areas.

Customer research is conducted to better understand their requirements and preferences.

Create buyer personas: Create buyer personas to help drive your marketing and sales activities.

Creating customer-focused products and services: Creating products and services that address the demands and preferences of your target market.

Understanding your target market and consumer needs allows you to produce products and services that fit their needs and preferences, enhancing your chances of success in the internet business.

Create a Sales Funnel and Marketing Strategy

Creating a sales funnel and marketing strategy is essential for growing a lucrative online business. This includes:

Creating a sales funnel involves guiding your customers through the purchasing process.

Creating a marketing strategy entails reaching your target market and driving traffic to your sales funnel.

Creating intriguing content: Creating material that appeals to your target market and increases conversions.

Optimize your sales funnel and marketing approach. Optimize your sales funnel and marketing plan to boost conversions and revenue.

You may enhance your internet business's earnings by creating a sales funnel and marketing strategy.

In this chapter, we looked at the key elements of starting a profitable online business, such as making a business plan and defining goals, evaluating target markets and customer demands, and developing a sales funnel and marketing strategy. By taking these steps, you can set a clear direction for your online business, develop products and services that fit the needs and preferences of your target market, and increase traffic and conversions.

Key Takeaways

Developing a business strategy and setting goals are critical for establishing a lucrative internet business.

Understanding your target market and client needs is critical for developing products and services that fulfill their expectations and preferences.

Creating a sales funnel and marketing strategy is critical to increasing traffic and conversions.

Action Items

Make a business strategy and establish financial targets for your online business.

Conduct market research to better understand your target market and their demands.

Create a sales funnel and marketing strategy to increase visitors and conversions.

Create captivating content that connects with your target audience and increases conversions.

Chapter 6: Mastering Affiliate Marketing

Welcome to the sixth chapter of "From Broke to Boss: The Complete Manual for Achieving Financial Independence Through Internet Revenue". In this chapter, we'll look at affiliate marketing basics, such as how to locate successful affiliate networks and create effective affiliate marketing campaigns.

Introduction to Affiliate Marketing

Affiliate marketing is a type of online marketing in which you promote items or services from other firms and earn a commission on sales. This includes:

Collaboration with businesses: Working together to market their products or services.

Earning commissions: Earning commissions on sales made using your unique affiliate link.

Product promotion entails promoting items or services through a variety of marketing channels, including social media, email marketing, and content marketing.

Affiliate marketing is a common way for internet marketers to make money, and it can be a profitable option for those who are ready to work hard to learn and succeed.

Find Profitable Affiliate Programs

Finding successful affiliate programs is critical to success in affiliate marketing. This includes:

Researching companies: Researching and assessing affiliate program providers' products or services.

Evaluating commission rates and payout structures to ensure their competitiveness.

Considering product demand: Taking into account product demand and popularity to ensure that the product is viable.

Looking for Affiliate Program Support: Looking for affiliate program support, such as tracking and reporting tools, to assist you with your affiliate marketing activities.

Finding profitable affiliate programs will boost your chances of success in affiliate marketing and earning more money.

Create Effective Affiliate Marketing Campaigns

Creating efficient affiliate marketing campaigns is critical to success in affiliate marketing. This includes:

Creating engaging content: Creating captivating material that promotes the product or service and speaks to your target audience.

To reach your target demographic, use a variety of marketing platforms such as social media, email marketing, and content marketing.

Developing a relationship with your audience: Developing a relationship with your target audience and developing trust to enhance conversion rates.

Tracking and improving your campaigns. Tracking and adjusting your campaigns to boost performance and conversions.

By developing successful affiliate marketing programs, you may boost your chances of success and earn more money.

In this chapter, we looked at affiliate marketing basics, such as how to locate successful affiliate networks and create effective affiliate marketing campaigns. Following these methods will boost your chances of success in affiliate marketing and earning more money.

Key Takeaways

Affiliate marketing is a type of online marketing in which you promote items or services from other firms and earn a commission on sales.

Finding successful affiliate programs is critical to success in affiliate marketing.

Creating efficient affiliate marketing campaigns is critical to success in affiliate marketing.

Action Items

Investigate affiliate program providers and assess their offerings.

Create intriguing material that promotes the product or service and appeals to your target audience.

Use different marketing platforms to reach your target demographic and boost conversions.

Track and optimize your campaigns for better performance and conversions.

Chapter 7: Selling Products and Services Online

Welcome to the seventh chapter of "From Broke to Boss: The Complete Manual for Achieving Financial Independence Through Internet Revenue". In this chapter, we'll look at how to sell things and services online, including an overview of e-commerce platforms and marketplaces, generating and selling digital products, and online service selling tactics.

An Overview of E-Commerce Platforms and Marketplaces

E-commerce platforms and marketplaces enable businesses to sell items and services online. This includes:

E-commerce platforms include Shopify, WooCommerce, and BigCommerce, which enable enterprises to construct their online stores.

Marketplaces: Websites such as Amazon, eBay, and Etsy allow businesses to offer their products and services to a huge number of customers.

The advantages of adopting e-commerce platforms and marketplaces include increased reach, simplicity of usage, and lower prices.

Understanding e-commerce platforms and marketplaces allows businesses to select the best solution for their needs and begin selling products and services online.

Developing and selling digital products

Digital items include ebooks, courses, and software. This includes:

Examples of digital items include ebooks, courses, software, and membership sites.

The advantages of selling digital products include reduced production costs, ease of distribution, and the potential for passive revenue.

Strategies for selling digital items include developing high-quality products, promoting successfully, and establishing a devoted consumer base.

Businesses can generate revenue while also building a devoted consumer base by developing and selling digital items.

Strategies for Selling Services Online:

Selling services online may be a significant source of income, particularly for firms that provide consulting, coaching, or freelance services. This includes:

Consulting, coaching, freelancing, and online tutoring are all services that can be sold online.

Benefits: Selling services online offers inexpensive initial costs, flexibility, and the possibility for large earnings.

Strategies for selling services online include establishing a strong online presence, effective marketing, and providing high-quality services.

Businesses can generate revenue while also developing a loyal consumer base by selling services online.

In this chapter, we looked at the world of online product and service sales, including an overview of e-commerce platforms and marketplaces, generating and selling digital products, and online service selling tactics. Businesses that implement these techniques can generate revenue while also building a loyal consumer base.

Key Takeaways

E-commerce platforms and marketplaces enable businesses to sell items and services online.

eBooks, courses, and software are examples of digital products that can be offered online.

Consulting, coaching, and freelancing are all services that can be sold online.

Action Items

Investigate e-commerce platforms and marketplaces to see which one is ideal for your business.

Create high-quality digital products that cater to the needs of your target market.

Create a strategy for selling services online that includes establishing a strong online presence and efficient marketing.

Chapter 8: Developing a Loyal Audience

Welcome to the eighth chapter of "From Broke to Boss: The Complete Manual for Achieving Financial Independence Through Internet Revenue". In this chapter, we'll look at why it's important to cultivate a devoted audience, how to do so, and how to engage with your audience and build trust.

Understanding the Importance of Creating a Loyal Audience

Creating a devoted audience is essential for any Internet business. This includes:

Increased sales: A loyal audience is more inclined to buy from you, which boosts sales and earnings.

Improved engagement: A committed audience is more inclined to interact with your content, share it, and provide feedback.

Better customer retention: A committed audience is more likely to stick with your business, lowering turnover and improving client lifetime value.

Building a dedicated audience allows you to increase revenue, improve engagement, and retain customers.

Strategies for Developing a Loyal Audience

There are various ways to create a loyal audience, including:

Email Marketing: Creating an email list and sending out regular newsletters to keep your audience engaged.

Social media: Using social media platforms to engage with your audience, share content, and develop relationships.

Material marketing entails creating high-quality, relevant, and valuable material to attract and engage your target audience.

Influencer marketing entails collaborating with influencers in your industry to reach a larger audience and establish trust.

Using these tactics, you may grow a devoted following and enhance interaction.

Tips for Engaging Your Audience and Building Trust

Building a devoted audience requires engaging with them and establishing trust. This includes:

Replying to comments and messages: Responding to comments and communications in a timely and personalized way.

Providing value: Adding value to your audience with high-quality material, tips, and resources.

Be real and transparent in your communication and marketing activities.

Showing appreciation: Expressing gratitude to your audience and honoring their loyalty.

Following these guidelines can help you engage with your audience, create trust, and increase loyalty.

This chapter has covered the necessity of developing a devoted audience, tactics for doing so, and recommendations for engaging with your audience and building trust. By implementing these methods and tips, you can establish a devoted audience and boost engagement.

Key Takeaways

Creating a devoted audience is essential for any Internet business.

Email marketing, social media, content marketing, and influencer marketing are all effective strategies for attracting a dedicated audience.

Responding to comments and messages, providing value, being real and upfront, and expressing gratitude are all good ways to engage your audience and establish trust.

Action Items

Create an email list and send out regular newsletters to keep your audience engaged.

Connect with your audience, share content, and establish relationships through social media channels.

Create high-quality, relevant, and valuable content to attract and engage your target audience.

Respond to comments and communications in a timely and personable manner.

Chapter 9: Increasing Your Online Income

Welcome to the ninth chapter of "From Broke to Boss: The Complete Manual for Achieving Financial Independence Through Internet Revenue". In this chapter, we'll look at tactics for increasing your internet income, recommendations for outsourcing and delegating activities, and tax and financial planning for online money.

Strategies for increasing your online income

Scaling your internet income necessitates a variety of tactics, including:

Paid advertising refers to using paid advertising channels such as Google AdWords, Facebook Ads, and native advertising to reach a larger audience.

Influencer marketing entails collaborating with influencers in your niche to promote your products or services to their audiences.

Material marketing entails creating high-quality, relevant, and valuable material to attract and engage your target audience.

Email marketing entails creating an email list and sending out regular newsletters to keep your audience interested and promote your products or services.

Using these tactics, you may increase your internet revenue and reach a larger audience.

Tips for Outsourcing and delegating tasks

As your internet business expands, you must outsource and delegate chores to free up your time and focus on high-value operations. This includes:

Identifying outsourcing tasks: Identifying outsourceable jobs such as content development, social media administration, and customer service.

Finding the proper people: Determine who to outsource jobs to, such as freelancers, virtual assistants, or agencies.

Setting clear expectations and rules for outsourced jobs is essential to ensuring quality and consistency.

Monitoring and Evaluation: Monitoring and analyzing the performance of outsourced tasks to ensure they meet your standards.

Outsourcing and delegating work allows you to free up time and focus on high-impact activities that promote development and income.

Understanding Taxation and Financial Planning for Online Income

As an online business owner, you must understand taxes and financial planning to maximize your earnings. This includes:

Taxes on Online Income: Understanding taxes on internet income, such as self-employment, sales, and income taxes.

Financial planning entails developing a budget, saving, and investing strategy to ensure long-term financial stability.

Record-keeping: Keeping accurate income and expense records is necessary for proper tax filing and financial planning.

Seeking Professional Advice: Seek professional counsel from a tax or financial advisor to ensure you're making sound judgments.

Understanding taxes and financial planning allows you to make sound decisions and maintain long-term financial stability.

In this chapter, we looked at ways to increase your online income, recommendations for outsourcing and delegating activities, and tax and financial planning for online money. Following these tactics and recommendations will help you increase your internet revenue, free up time, and secure long-term financial stability.

Key Takeaways

Paid advertising, influencer marketing, content marketing, and email marketing are all effective strategies for increasing your online income.

Tips for outsourcing and delegating jobs include determining which tasks to outsource, locating the proper individuals, creating clear expectations, and monitoring and evaluating performance.

Understanding taxes and financial planning for online income is critical to long-term financial stability.

Action Items

Use paid advertising methods to attract a larger audience and increase your online revenue.

Collaborate with influencers in your niche to market your products or services to their audiences.

Outsource and delegate duties to free up time and concentrate on high-impact initiatives.

Seek professional counsel from a tax or financial advisor to ensure you're making sound judgments.

Chapter 10: Maintaining Financial Freedom

Welcome to the tenth and final chapter of "From Broke to Boss: The Complete Manual for Achieving Financial Independence Through Internet Revenue". In this chapter, we'll look at strategies for maintaining financial freedom, tips for avoiding financial pitfalls and staying motivated, and conclude with some final thoughts.

Strategies to Maintain Financial Freedom

Maintaining financial freedom requires ongoing effort and discipline. This includes:

Continuing education: Continuing to educate yourself on personal finance, investing, and online business to stay ahead of the curve.

Diversifying your income streams can help reduce risk and increase financial stability.

Budgeting and saving: Creating a budget and saving regularly to achieve long-term financial stability.

Investing wisely: Investing wisely in assets that align with your financial goals and risk tolerance.

By following these strategies, you can maintain financial freedom and achieve long-term financial stability.

Tips for Avoiding Financial Pitfalls and Staying Motivated

Avoiding financial pitfalls and remaining motivated necessitate discipline and self-awareness. This includes:

Avoiding debt and high-interest loans can help reduce financial stress.

Staying disciplined: Staying disciplined and focused on your financial goals helps avoid distractions and stay inspired.

Building an emergency fund: Building an emergency fund to cover unexpected expenses and avoid financial stress.

Celebrating milestones: Celebrating milestones and achievements to stay motivated and encouraged.

By following these suggestions, you can avoid financial pitfalls and stay motivated to reach your financial objectives.

Conclusion and Final Thoughts

In conclusion, gaining financial freedom through online income involves dedication, hard work, and discipline. By following the strategies and tips outlined in this guide, you can create a life of financial freedom and live the life you've always wanted.

Remember, financial freedom is a journey, not a destination. It requires ongoing effort and discipline, but the rewards are well worth it.

We hope this guide has equipped you with the knowledge and inspiration you need to attain financial freedom through online income. We wish you the best of luck on your journey to financial freedom.

Key Takeaways

Continuing education, income diversification, budgeting and saving, and wise investing are all strategies for maintaining financial freedom.

Avoiding debt, remaining disciplined, saving for an emergency, and celebrating achievements are all good ways to stay motivated and avoid financial problems.

Financial freedom involves continual effort and discipline, but the rewards are well worth it.

Action Items

Continue to educate yourself on personal finance, investing, and online business to stay ahead of the curve.

Diversify your revenue streams to reduce risk and boost financial stability.

Create a budget and save regularly to maintain long-term financial stability.

Invest sensibly in assets that align with your financial goals and risk tolerance.